CAÑON de los ARTISTAS

by Austin Deuel

WRITTEN, ORIGINAL PAINTINGS,
PHOTOGRAPHY, DRAWINGS AND SCULPTURE
BY

Austin Deuel

PUBLISHED BY DESERT WIND PUBLICATIONS

PUBLISHED IN THE UNITED STATES OF AMERICA
DESERT WIND PUBLICATIONS, INC.
7534 EAST 1st STREET
SCOTTSDALE, ARIZONA 85251

DEDICATION

I dedicate this book to Dr. Duncan Poth for giving me his great support and for making it possible to share this experience with so many.

To Jose,
may all your trails be down hill.

ILLUSTRATIONS

Map Of Baja California, *watercolor*   XIII
Highway Of The Gods, *oil*   3
Last Of The Californios, *bronze*   5
Heading For The Summit, *watercolor*   7
Transportation Gap, *watercolor*   9
Checking The Windsock, Clearing The Runway, *watercolor*   13
Last Light At San Francisco, *watercolor*   15
Supplies For San Ignacio, *bronze*   17
Letter From Walter, *oil*   19
Patient Wait, *oil*   21
Trail Companions, *bronze*   22
Staying In The Shade, *oil*   23
A Moment Of Peace, *watercolor*   24
More Shade Than Grass, *watercolor*   25
Ojeba Arce, *oil*   27
Starting For Town, *watercolor*   30
Milking Time At Guadalupe, *watercolor*   31
Thinning The Herd, *oil*   33
Packing For Guadalupe, *watercolor*   35
Water Break, *watercolor*   37
Morning Chores, *oil*   39
Pass The Rope Por Favor, *oil*   41
Changing Their Minds, *watercolor*   43
El Cacariso Cave And Juan, *oil*   45
Flechas Cave, 1384, *oil*   46, 47
Loading El Diablo, *bronze*   49
Canyon Crossing, *oil*   50
Leading The Way, *oil*   51
Juan And Poncho, *watercolor*   53
Dangerous Footing, *oil*   55
Pasa Por Favor, *oil*   57
Moving Out, *oil*   58
Needed Encouragement, *watercolor*   59
Dinner At Cueva Pintada, *watercolor*   61
Grandmother's Time, *oil*   63
Widow Of San Gregorio, *oil*   65
Tanning At San Gregorio, *watercolor*   67
The Flume At San Gregorio, *watercolor*   69
Adjusting The Cinch, *oil*   71
El Diablo, *bronze*   72
Heading For The Bottom, *watercolor*   73
Late Arrival, *watercolor*   75
Boojum Tree Country, *oil*   77

INTRODUCTION

I have been traveling to Baja California for twenty years with a great interest in and fascination for its stark beauty and the strong character of the living things, found few other places in the world, that survive in its extreme environment.

Prior to my deeper penetration of its borders, I had my first view of Baja through my visits to Tijuana as a young marine. At night I found myself blinded by its bright lights that covered the filth and degradation with their continuous blinking of red and yellow rays of neon. Only the light of day brought back the true perspective of what it really was: many unfortunate people doing anything to survive, at great expense to themselves. They were drawn to Tijuana from the harsh interiors of Mexico by rumors of money and greater chance for a higher standard of living. Also, living closer to the U.S. border meant easier access to the United States. Their lack of skills for city life and their country innocence made them easy prey for the hardened city dwellers who had preceded them. Having their destiny controlled by their desperation and loneliness, without friends or family to help, eroded their dignity and character. Tijuana has improved much since my first visit 25 years ago, but this sad style of life is still displayed to many visitors. Today, unfortunately, many Americans see men and women selling the only thing they came to this new life with: themselves. To the untraveled American, this becomes their first and lasting impression of Baja.

The "Baja Bug" is more than a car. It is also an infectious fever to experience Baja that has infected thousands of Americans. Many have raced its unforgiving deserts, sailed its majestic coastline of many-colored moods, flown over its moonlike surface that never seems to end — creating a love affair that becomes more intense with each new hour of exposure.

My friends and I have spent many a night around campfires in such unusual places of sound and beauty. The conversation always centers on the magnificent experiences we have had, past and present, on this exotic peninsula. We felt like the great discoverers of the past and relished our moments, knowing they have been experienced by only a daring few.

I have watched Baja change in the last twenty years,

although not as fast as some other remote areas of the earth, but I know that it is now on the edge of a great explosion of change. I have tried, in this book, to capture some of the ways that have not changed dramatically in a hundred years. A landscape that has avoided man's wrath for millions of years. Man is now starting to put gas in his little engines, and has begun to tear at a surface that took millions of years to create. As in any love affair, it will change and I am going to be terribly sad about my inability to return to certain areas and see them the way they were when I visited them before.

I do wish for a better life and standard of living for the inhabitants of this great country. At present it is a harsh existence for many of its dwellers. But I do hope that while making changes man is aware of the value of this area and protects some of its natural beauty and unique treasures, such as these cave paintings found nowhere else in the world, except China, in such concentration and size. Some of the cave paintings are as old as nine hundred years, painted by the descendents of the original inhabitants of this amazing country. They represent the only significant evidence of a people's existence and their culture, except for arrowheads found in the region. There are no buildings, graveyards, baskets or written material to prove their existence — only these cave paintings.

The Spanish came looking for gold in the middle 1700's, and attempted to civilize and convert the inhabitants to the Catholic church. They only succeeded in wiping them out totally with diseases they had brought with them from Europe. Man's next attack on what little is left of the records of this civilization and its very existence will be by those people who destroy and litter, through immaturity and ignorance of the things they see before their eyes. These treasures are irreplaceable and should be allowed their natural death of time.

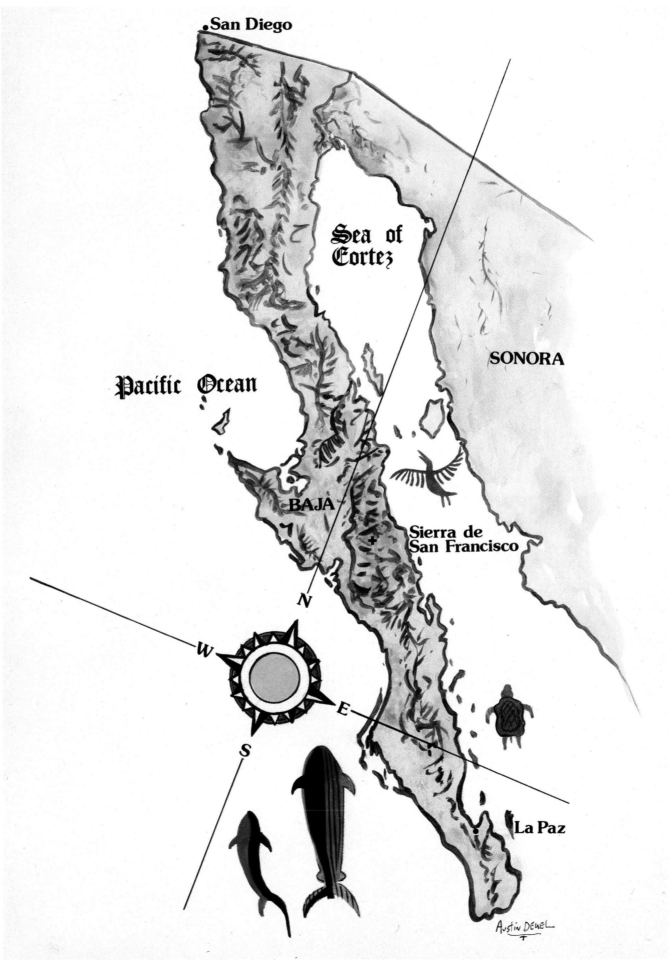

San Diego

Sea of Cortez

Pacific Ocean

SONORA

BAJA

Sierra de
San Francisco

N

W

E

S

La Paz

Austin Dewel

Map Of Baja California

The most consistently unclouded, clearly visible detail of North America seen from an orbiting space vehicle is a slender, misshapen finger of land dangling from the southwest corner of the continental mass, a peninsula called Baja (Lower) California. It is longer than Italy, has more than a thousand miles of shoreline, and contains 55,000 square miles of almost empty wilderness. Located at about the half-way point of Baja is a sierra or mountain called Sierra San Francisco, its canyons and arroyas carved by forgotten torrents that ended in a dry alluvial fan on the desert floor below.

These canyon walls safeguard an art treasure created by artists who lived approximately 800 to 900 years ago, art which can never be shipped to any museum in the world. It's an art show without spotlights, invitations, tuxedos, critics or champagne in little plastic glasses. The paintings are in their original frames created by Mother Nature's daily moods and light, accented by nature's own soundtrack, and painted on man's oldest canvas -- rock. You are still able to see the artists' palettes located at the base of their paintings and impregnated with the colors used in their creations. The caretakers of this fine collection of art are mountain people living in the 20th century by 19th century means. They have a great appreciation of their artistic inheritance, and their old ways accent its beauty and history.

In the mid-18th century, when California still meant only a peninsula and many thought of it as an island, two or three Jesuit missionaries, toiling in the rockiest of vineyards, made surprising finds of ancient art. During the next two centuries their little-known discovery was augmented at long intervals, first by a French chemist stationed at Santa Rosalia to oversee a copper strike the French made in the late 1800's and then, almost a hundred years later, by a 20th century American writer of detective fiction.

The Jesuits' early contact in the mid-1750's was cut short by their expulsion a decade later, when most non-Spanish missionaries were retired to their homelands, barred from Spain and all her possessions. Those of Spanish extraction were placed under Papal care and were largely concentrated at Bologna. These Jesuits, with their frontier spirit and efforts to spread the ways of Catholic Christianity, had been most active in the Baja area and produced the first written records of its sights and culture.

The greatest concentration of cave paintings is located north of San Ignacio in a mountain wilderness known as Sierra de la San Francisco. The largest of the many cave paintings located here were first introduced to the modern world by an expedition mounted in 1962 by the writer Erle Stanley Gardner.

In 1962 Gardner, creator of Perry Mason and other fictional sleuths, got wind of a very large cave containing remarkable primitive paintings located somewhere in the Sierras of Baja California. He decided to do some sleuthing of his own and organized an expedition to search out the exact location of the cave.

Sam Hicks of Temecula, California, was a member of this party which flew into the Sierras where its members learned of the cave paintings of Lacueva Pintada. The local people described a giant *cueve* or cave far down the Arroya de San Pablo. Flying back to tell the others in the party of this revelation, they took the route described to them by the people of the village of San Francisco. By good fortune Hicks spotted the cave from the air, and they were able to land their helicopter and take a few pictures. Seeing the photos convinced Gardner that he was on to something big, and he organized the return expedition with Dr. Meighan. Nat Farbman of Life Magazine was also in the party, which led to national coverage of the discovery and generated universal, although brief, interest.

This area is scarred by large volcanic outpourings rising up from the surrounding desert floor to heights of more than five thousand feet. It covers an area thirty miles from north to south and half that distance from east to west. From its center and mesas you have an eagle's view west to Scammon's Lagoon and the Vizcaino Desert. The Sierra's great canyons of multi-colored rock, with a variety of vegetation clinging to their fortress-like walls, accentuate the sounds of the resident wildlife. The canyon bottoms are covered with smooth rock, reflecting centuries of water passage. Quiet pools of clear water are scattered under the surprisingly many palm groves that wind their way up these snakelike canyons to the top of the mesa, with small ranchos located at the more permanent water holes.

This trip was to be an experience of wonderment and joy for me and my friends, affording us an opportunity to touch a living form of the 19th century basically untouched by the

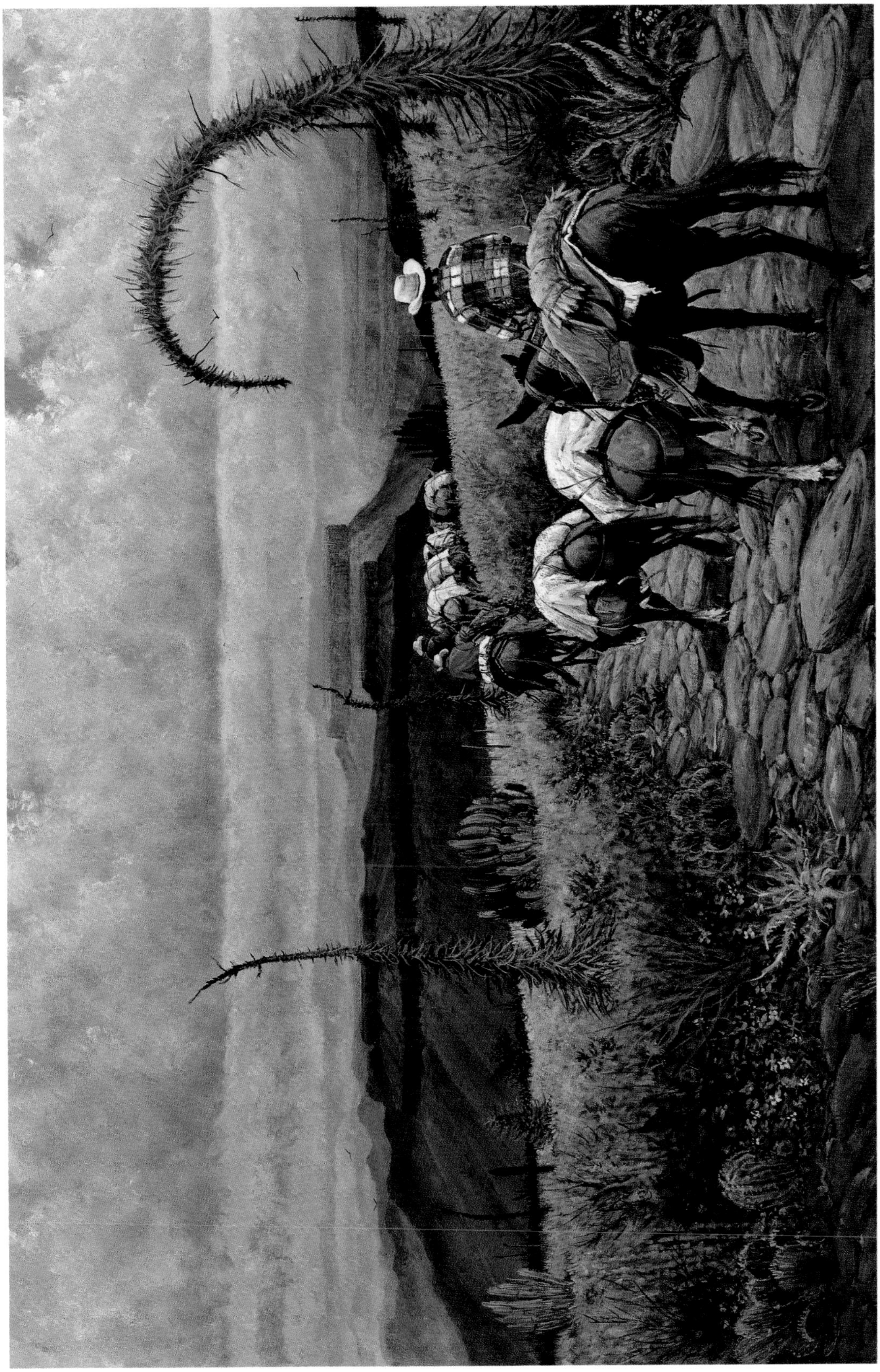

Highway Of The Gods

20th. These people are the last of the Californios, native in race and culture. They are a gentle people in a hard land, using the old ways taught to them by their forefathers. Accenting the beauty of the intriguingly rough, rock land are many plants found nowhere else in the world. Cave paintings of equal magnitude and number are known to exist only in one other spot on the globe, China.

I found out about this place through conversations with Klaus Schilling, a good friend since before our manhood. Klaus had read of these people and their cave paintings in some of Harry Crosby's writings about the area, and we became interested in having the personal experience for ourselves. Klaus' father, a doctor who had spent much of his free time over the years traveling to Baja by air and VW bug, was fascinated by these people and their land. Dr. Schilling had personally spoken with and gotten to know some of the people while giving them medical assistance in the past, so we had some inside connections.

The men I was traveling with, five in all, have had many experiences worldwide. Among us, we have probably logged over a million miles of travel, seeking new worlds, new forms of beauty, and many other ways of thought and lifestyle which we seek to touch personally because of our great appreciation for past and present.

Three of my companions I had known a long time before this adventure. Pat Pritchard I met at the beginning of our first trip and he was to make all six of them with us. His traveling experiences included Europe, Africa, the South Pacific and other far corners of the earth. He was somewhat handicapped by contact lenses which, because of all the dust and dirt on our rough journey, caused his eyes to become inflamed. They also cost the rest of us much time on our hands and knees looking for the elusive lens that got away more than once.

Austin WEKEL

Last Of The Californios

Klaus Schilling and I met as very young men and have been in and out of each other's life for well over 20 years. He was born in Germany and came to America after the second world war. He has traveled back to his homeland many times and toured Europe down to Greece, as well as South America, satisfying his interest in the anthropology and history of our globe. On our trips to Baja he would trade in his banker's suit and tie, buckle on leather leggings like those worn by the Californios, and climb on a mule for the long, hard journey. But when the rest of us were tired and ready to quit he would revert to his executive manner and get the last mile out of us.

His father, Dr. Walter Schilling, was a different part of my life as a young man when I dated one of his nieces, sent here as a foreign exchange student from Germany. I would sit at his large formal dining table in Pasadena where German was the only language spoken. Although my heritage is Germanic, I didn't understand a word, and when Walter's mother-in-law lectured me harshly on the proper way to handle the dating of her granddaughter, in German of course, I had to hope I got all my head movements in acknowledgement of her "do's and don'ts" in the right places.

7

Heading For The Summit

Walter was born in Guatemala and moved to Germany as a young boy at the outbreak of the first world war when Guatemala exercised a program of deporting German citizens as a war protest. He was in the German army during the second world war where his experiences included time on the Russian front and two years in one of our prisoner-of-war camps. He was released at the end of the war and, due to his Guatemalan citizenship as well as to much effort on his part, was able to secure passage for himself and his family to the United States. Once here he completed the requirements to become a medical doctor. He is the only person I have ever been in the bush with who wears cotton pajamas to bed every night whatever his surroundings. But he was our cook and a damn good one, so we couldn't make too much fun of him.

I met Pat Waters in a sign painting shop owned by a good friend of mine in Escondido, California. He was 19 at the time and had expressed great interest in learning to paint, so I began helping where I could in this respect. He was the youngest member of our group and because of his crop-dusting experiences earned, along with me, the berth of piloting the chase plane in our Baja adventures. He has traveled Baja much, flown his Super Cub to Alaska and Canada, and has many hours of wilderness flying to his credit, a fact which I know saved my life on at least one occasion in Baja.

That particular experience was a big lesson to all of us. After a great many years of flying over the Baja peninsula, we had become used to its vastness and complacent about its remoteness and the ruggedness of the terrain beneath us. When something finally went wrong it was a much needed lesson to secure our well-being for continued travel in the area.

The unwanted adventure began about three o'clock in the morning when we were brought out of our sleep by a sudden gust of wind that made the plane lunge at its tie-down ropes attached to the wings we were sleeping under.

We had flown in that afternoon for an overnight stop, to have dinner with our friends and make arrangements for our next trip to the caves, planning to fly on to Mulege the next day for their Saturday night pig roast. Our attire, although informal, was geared for that social event, not for camping or hiking in the wilderness. We had the wrong shoes and no change of clothing, certainly nothing warm. Furthermore, we

had only one canteen of water for all of us, and no food -- just the memory of a glorious meal with wine the night before.

Our plane's design was very marginal for this airstrip, and one magneto was breaking up which makes for less than a full power situation. We knew from the beginning of our trip that we could not take all three of us out in a single take-off. The runway was too short and soft for our combined weight to be safe under the best of conditions. We planned to run a shuttle from San Francisco to Santa Rosalita, taking out one person at a time; that way we would be on an airstrip that could easily handle the fully loaded plane. With proper conditions, we should have had no problem implementing this plan, but with that opening gust the winds of trouble started blowing our way.

The temperature had dropped considerably by first light, and an intermittent rain began to fall. We were socked in. The rain stopped as the morning wore on, but we still had the clouds and a terrible crosswind. We used our last water for coffee that we drank huddled around the campfire, using its warmth to make up for our lack of clothing while we waited for the clouds to lift. This was when we began to feel very stupid and all too aware of the distance between us and any kind of help. But, still thinking weather was our only problem, we clung to one last bit of dignity in our pride. The weather was breaking up, and we could see our way out even though there was still a strong crosswind.

I woke up Pat who was sleeping in the plane and announced that the clouds had lifted sufficiently for a take-off. We loaded our sleeping bags. Klaus and Pat were going first, then Pat would come back and get me. With an 1800-foot runway, the plane had to take off uphill to get the right angle of the crosswind. They warmed up the plane and taxied down to the end of the runway where I pulled the tail of the plane back into the brush to give them maximum use of the runway. Pat revved the engine, holding on the brake, and away they went -- but it wasn't going to work and he had to abort the take-off.

He tried a few more times, but there just wasn't enough power to lift the weight. So we talked it over for a while, then decided to try it with just Pat and the camping gear, and if he could lift off he was to fly to the point of San Francisco and try to find another plane that would get us out. Klaus and I pulled the tail back into the brush, then Pat made another run at it.

He barely got airborne before the end of the runway but, having to go uphill, he was skimming along only a scary few feet above the ground and lifted his landing gear just in time to miss the brush and the rock wall that was located a few hundred yards past the lift-off point. Dropping behind that, he was out of sight. We held our breath, straining for sight or sound of him, until he finally lifted up into our view again and, to our great relief, headed for a safe altitude.

We anxiously awaited his return, Klaus and I discussing our predicament and the possibility of a three-day overland trip to get out of it. We spoke of the condition we would be in when we finally arrived in San Ignacio -- and the laughter we would hear from the other end of the phone when we told his father about our stupid lack of preparedness for this trip. But then, a few hours later, we heard the drone of a small plane coming toward us. Our spirits lifted -- until we saw it was the same plane.

Pat landed and got out to tell us there were no suitable planes at point of San Francisco and, even if there were, all available pilots were too far into their cups to assist us. So he had left our camping gear there, figuring that with the load lightened by that much plus the fuel he'd burned off, he might be able to make it with Klaus, 75 pounds lighter than me, as a passenger. Then, having burned off more fuel, he'd come back for me.

We still had that strong crosswind to deal with and it had to be an uphill take-off again. We decided to let Pat try it once by himself to see if it would be any better than his first attempt at lift-off. So once again Klaus and I pulled the plane's tail back into the brush, then away he went, lifting off much more easily this time although it was still far from ideal. He came back around and landed. We loaded Klaus aboard and returned to the take-off position, all aware that this was going to be close. With the engine revved to peak RPMs, Pat stood on the brakes for the moment of commitment. Then the plane lunged forward, showering me with dust and rocks as it headed up the runway for the point of no return. It finally lifted off, struggling for every inch of altitude and settling for a second to give my heart a twinge. But it regained its composure, skimmed over the rock wall and started gaining altitude. Now I was alone. Klaus had left me his watch so I would have some way of knowing whether Pat would return for me that day. It was

13

already late in the afternoon and if he wasn't back in an hour he would have to wait until morning.

Time dragged slowly as the light faded into the west. Then, with great relief, I heard the sound of a far-off engine and soon Pat landed. The wind was still intense and blowing in the same direction -- if it would only change, making a downhill take-off possible, it would relieve a lot of the pressure. Pat paced back and forth, knowing this last lift-off would, because of my weight, be an even greater invitation to catastrophe than the earlier ones despite his having burned off more fuel to lighten the load. He looked my way and I said, "Well, you've made it over the wall three times -- let's go for four!"

We couldn't take any longer to make a decision because we were running out of light. We pulled the plane back as far as we could, then we both jumped in and tugged at our seatbelts. We went through the final checklist, looked at each other, then went for it. Both pairs of eyes were watching to see if we'd attain air speed, a seemingly impossible goal. We passed the no-return point on the runway still just short of it. We both looked straight ahead -- no use looking anywhere else now. Pat pulled up the landing gear, which I swear gave us our only altitude at that point, and we clipped the tops of the bushes at the end of the runway. At this point, the hardest thing for a pilot to do is not follow your instinct to pull back on the wheel -- which would just create a stall and that would be all she wrote. Pat started to say, "We're going in . . . ." and was preparing for it when all of a sudden the plane began to grip the air and gain altitude.

We cleared the wall. Pat and I shook hands and I said, "Well, we beat the grim reaper again." Pat said, "Yeah, the last time I was in a spot like that I crashed." But our moment of relief was shattered as we looked at the gas gauges. Both needles were on empty, one completely dead and the other moving only slightly when Pat jiggled the plane. "I may have cut this too close," he said, and I replied that he had better take the quickest route to the coast since it would be better to spend a wet night on the beach than to try our luck in this rough country.

We made directly for the coast, then turned toward our final destination. We were losing light fast and Baja airstrips don't have landing lights, so we were running out of time as well as gas. We could see our destination, but it was still more than

ten minutes away and now both gas needles were completely stationary. Needless to say, it was a very long ten minutes. We landed with the last possible light and pulled up to the fueling area. I got out, turned to Pat and said, "Don't fill it up -- I don't want to know how close it was." With that we quickly removed ourselves to the bar where we made a heartfelt request -- "Tequila, por favor!"

Fortunately, we had no crystal ball to foretell some of the grim adventures that would be coming our way in the next six years of travel to this remote area of Baja when we started planning our first expedition. Having agreed on a time, Klaus and his dad began making the necessary arrangements for the arduous trip to the Baja cave paintings. It would take months of preparation. Supplies from the United States had to be flown to a staging area that had airplane fuel and storage as close as possible to our destination. This turned out to be Point San Friscisqito, located at the edge of the Gulf of California, more than 300 miles below the border. There they kept our camping and food supplies until we were ready to move them to the high country village of the central Baja mountains.

Supplies For San Ignacio

The guides in the village were alerted by letter. The letter, handwritten by Walter who speaks and writes fluent Spanish, gave the date and time of our arrival. These instructions had to be sent well in advance as it took weeks to get to the village. The guides had to arrange for extra mules and burros for our trek, and also make arrangements to have their ranch duties covered by other family members or friends while they were gone. All the ranches and villages are dependent on mutual cooperation for reasonable survival in such a primitive area.

In the Spring we were finally flying toward this high mountain village in the center of Baja. We flew down the Sea of Cortez with its abrupt cliffs and jagged rocks edged by a gentle emerald-green surf that foamed white as it made contact with the foreboding land. The cliffs, dark red and brown marbled with blacks, ochres and tans, vegetation seemingly non-existent from the air, are set off against a very visible, abundant sea life in the clear waters offshore. This is land of great contrasts and colors.

As we drew closer to the center of the Baja mountain range, heading for its highest visible peak, we began to see below us trails on the sides of mountains and along canyon walls, worn by years of travel on foot and by mule. It had taken us, after turning in from the coast, a little over 20 minutes to cover the same distance that takes three days by mule.

As the high peak loomed in front of us we spotted the first village at its base, an altitude of slightly over 5,000 feet. Our excitement mounted as we began looking for the primitive airstrip nearby, then we circled and started our descent. The strip, appearing out of nowhere below, had been cleared and maintained by the villagers using just basic hand tools and their great collective effort, but it is still only for planes designed for the roughest landing conditions. We traveled in two planes which is the safest practice in the remoteness of the Baja interiors, where there is no radio contact with the ground for wind conditions, altimeter settings and such. A windsock, beat-up and full of holes, flew from the top of a spindly tree -- if you could find it at all from the air.

The first plane made a low pass over the field, checking for any possible ground damage left unrepaired after the last rainstorm -- also to chase the goats and burros off the runway before final approach and landing. Pat and I were in the

19

Letter From Walter

second plane, his Super Cub which is perfect for these primitive conditions. We watched from above, tuned to the other plane's radio frequency, until it made a successful landing, then followed it down, coming in low over the heads of the men and youths of the village. Even on subsequent visits, after they knew us well, they still kept their women from our sight and from participating in the greetings at the airstrip.

The runway is located between two very small villages, Guadalupe and San Francisco, the latter bearing the same name as the mountain range. They were as different in their appearance as in their names. One was neat and showed pride of ownership, while the other was sloppy and unkempt. It showed me that out of reach of government influence and formal education there still was a level of extra pride and effort in one and not the other. I'm sure there were neat caves and unkempt caves during the caveman era. So some men do have a natural pride of ownership. It must be a natural instinct and one of the signs of competitiveness among men that helps them move forward in the evolution of their living habits in spite of present living conditions.

The villagers' main exports are goat cheese and hides. This commerce gives them money to buy staples such as salt, flour and sugar, as well as some clothes. They make their own shoes. I watched a young man in the village put his foot on a piece of cardboard, then draw a line around the outer edge to make a pattern of his foot. Placing the pattern on a piece of tire, he used a knife to cut out the soles for a shoe. He then took a piece of goat hide for the heel section and nailed it to the tire sole; a second piece of hide was nailed to the front for the toe section. He punched two pairs of holes, then made shoelaces out of a rawhide string. The entire operation took 20 minutes -- less time than it takes to buy a pair of shoes in your neighborhood shopping mall.

The nearest trading town for them is three days by mule down a long, rocky trail. It is a typical small Mexican town, with mostly dirt streets and limited electricity, called San Inacio.

These high country villagers are a gentle people, wise in the ways of living off the land, their ways unchanged in over a hundred years. Their life is simple and basic. Houses are simply stones piled to a height of about four feet with a wooden frame above that, the whole topped by a roof of local vegetation, then thatched with palm leaves collected in the canyons below and transported to the top of the mesa -- a task consuming many long, weary hours. They also have some very basic plywood houses with concrete floors -- all the materials brought in on burros from the town below in an effort to upgrade their homes. But it is a very slow process due to the difficulty of transporting the building supplies.

Trail Companions

23

Staying In The Shade

Each rancho or small village has a leader, usually the elder of the first family to settle in the area, who directs everyone else in their daily tasks. Ojeba Arce, the old gentleman who ran this village of about 30 people, was in his 70's when I first met him more than five years ago, but still very spry and hard-working. The first impression I had of him was that of a mystic. The brisk wind blowing over the mesa turned his white hair into a disheveled halo, made brilliant by the bright morning sun which also accentuated the contrast between flashing hair and golden brown face. The wrinkles of time, showing the extent of his exposure both to the elements and to hardship, told the story of this man's life very well without his saying a word.

The villagers raise about twenty-five hundred goats and some cattle, but not as many of the latter as they did 20 years ago. The land has become more arid and suffers from many years of overgrazing, so goats are the only animals adaptable to present range conditions. They also have a complement of burros and mules to transport their export and bring needed outside supplies up from below. A few chickens, turkeys and pigs are in evidence, but on the whole they look to be a pretty sickly lot.

The goats have to be milked every day and the whole village takes part in this task which is carried out in the goat pens. These are made of the local brush, trees and rock, with the thorny brush adding to the efficiency of what would otherwise be a rather flimsy corral. The villagers move through the herd in a stooped position, snatching up a hind leg after feeling a full udder and filling their small pails quickly. Village children then gather up the milked ewes, giving them the old heave-ho over the corral fence and later driving them off to the hills to graze. The small kids are kept in the corral, where they cry piteously for their mothers all day long -- thus insuring that the mothers won't run too far off during the day and will return in the evening.

As the milking process and subsequent expulsion thins out the corral population the remaining ewes, with more freedom to elude the quick hands of their pursuers, become increasingly more difficult to catch. Now, changing their method of pursuit, the young men bring into action brightly colored nylon ropes that have hung limp in their hands. The strong yellows and blues of these ropes, contrasting with the somber

Ojeba Arce

Starting For Town

31

Milking Time At Guadalupe

earth tones of dried brush, leather and stone, seem very much out of place here, but the youngsters handle them with grace and speed to rope the uncooperative ewes. I'm used to our cowboys' more rigid rope with a surer loop appearing in hand before the toss, and am sure these kids could rope a grasshopper on the fly.

A hundred goats, give or take a few, can produce 30 to 40 gallons of milk a day. A large storage bucket is set near the corrals with a damp rag placed over it to keep out the dust. Individual milkers fill this and others like it from their smaller buckets. The milk is then carried to one of the houses in the village to start the process of turning it into goat cheese for export to the outside world. The kitchen area of the house has been tidied to allow adequate space, and all utensils to be used have been freshly washed. If the cheesemaker is one of those who has just engaged in milking, he or she changes outer garments and scrubs up thoroughly. Clean cheese is a matter of both pride and of economics. The surroundings are primitive but, under the circumstances, the general cleanliness is very good.

Traditionally, the cheesemaking process began by adding scrapings from the dried after-stomach of a deer or cow to the fresh milk. The scraped substance, called rennet in English, contains rennin, an enzyme which curdles milk. Today, however, a purer, tinned product is used on many ranches for convenience and more uniform results. The milk curdles very rapidly, and in less than ten minutes the cheesemaker begins to use a large strainer to lift out semi-solid curds which are placed gently in a V-shaped, wooden trough with a crack at the bottom to allow the liquid whey to drain into a pan below. After a half-hour or so, the curd in the trough solidifies to a point at which it can be sliced, the slices salted, then crumbled by hand as the salt is kneaded in.

At this point the cheese acquires its characteristic form, a somewhat flattened rectangular block or loaf. Each rancher has constructed a dozen or more stout little baskets, about 15 inches high, made from straight stalks of an arroyo bush called *guatomote*. These are bound together in log-cabin fashion, using rawhide lashing at the corners and edges. Each container is lined with a clean cloth, then packed with firm but moist milk curd. When the basket is full, the cloth is folded neatly over the top, then covered with a piece of wood

which just fits into the basket form. This board is used to squeeze the cheese inside the cloth, pressing it tightly into form. Larger cheeses require so much pressure that those who make them have constructed ingenious presses capable of exerting a hundred pounds or more of pressure on the cheese.

After a few hours, a day at the most, the cheese is removed from both forms and warppings and placed on racks suspended up out of the way in the high gable of the kitchen or storeroom. There it will cure and dry for a few days until the rind is tough enough to hold up under the strenuous trip to market. In a good year cheesemaking continues from October through April, and provides each family with the cash and credit needed for their growing lists of items to be purchased. Profit as well as work is shared by all. It is a cooperative system in each village or rancho.

The first time I sampled this local cheese I didn't care for it, but as the years have gone by I've acquired a taste for its unique flavor.

But these were things we learned as we got to know the villagers better over the years. On that first visit, after exchanging greetings on the airstrip, we began unloading supplies from our 20th century motorized bird onto a small, four-legged creature of a breed used as beast of burden since thousands of years before Christ -- the burro. Then, with our guide's assistance, we began to saddle a slightly more contemporary mode of travel -- the mule -- for our trip to the village of Guadalupe where we would pick up more animals and finish packing our supplies.

As we worked, the few women in sight were going down a very steep trail to a waterhole, their only source of water for every purpose from washing clothes to drinking both by man and beast. From my viewpoint, the water looked like split pea soup due to the heavy algae content, certainly not very appetizing. The women would fill their buckets and, one in each hand, start back up the hill, never stopping until they reached their houses at the top. Conditions are very rough for women in these hills. Also, there are more men than women. A few men have been lucky enough to find women in the towns below who will return to the hills with them, but these are the exceptions. Most of the women who are born here don't stay.

After a few hours we had finished loading all the animals and were growing more and more anxious to move off on our adventure. The feelings of that first trip were very special to us. The appreciation was always there on later trips, but never again was there that nervousness about the unknown coupled with great anticipation. I felt as though I had bought a map to King Solomon's Mine on the dark side of the continent, with a promise of great riches and joy coming my way.

With everything loaded and all straps and ropes tightened until there was no slack, we mounted and moved off on our

20th century journey into a 19th century land. Juan and Poncho, our main guides, were proud men. These people are, by and large, of Spanish descent and handsome to look at. There is no living evidence of the Indians who once roamed this land in great numbers. They were rendered totally extinct by the arrival of the Spanish in the 16th century, mostly because of exposure to diseases brought by the foreigners.

Juan and Poncho showed great appreciation for the rugged beauty of their country, and very much appreciated the fact that we were equally enthralled by the land's magical appeal.

They loaded their animals each morning as routinely as we start our cars and drive off to work. But instead of stepping out to a carport, each dawn they went in search of the animals that had been hobbled and turned loose the night before. In the clear morning air we could hear them coming toward camp, the animals' neck bells clanging in rhythm as they arrived with steam blowing from their nostrils and rising off their backsides. We waved them into a huddled bunch to quiet down and await the day's task. Juan and Poncho began to rope the ones they wanted to load first, starting with the burros. They clambered over the never-ending rocks in their home-made shoes with great agility, ropes dangling limply from their hands. Picking out the beast they wanted, they'd give a quick flick of the wrist -- got him! Then they'd lead the burro over to a pile of supplies, pulling and tugging at endless ropes, balancing the load, exchanging gentle conversation all the while. Their grace and ease of movement as they went about their tasks in the cool morning breeze was fascinating to watch.

As in every string of trail or working animals, there were some that were green, others hard to handle. These animals had a wide blown band added to the halter; this could be pulled down over the eyes to get their attention and cooperation, and when it was in place they would stand perfectly still until fully loaded or saddled. Padding for the packing tree was made of goat hide pieces sewn together to form a bag that was stuffed with straw, with a breaching strap sewn to that. They made a packing cinch strap out of a strip of tire rubber. A hole in one end was threaded with a long piece of rope that had a hand-carved wooden hook at the end. This was slung under the burro to the other packer, and the tightening process began.

After packing the burros, our guides proceeded to saddle the mules. Juan's personal mount was a beauty -- black, young and not completely broken, so we had the usual morning rodeo like cowboys anywhere at their day's beginning. After some effort and a great deal of agility on Juan's part, he got the brow band pulled down over the mule's eyes and there was no further movement until after the saddling. They used much more padding than I was used to seeing because of the extreme "ups and downs" of this country. The saddle is placed on, with a machete and rifle scabbard added. Over this goes a large piece of leather that covers the entire saddle from the top, with built-in saddlebags in front. This gives added protection from the harsh plant life of the trail. Tied to the back of the saddle is a big leather bag to carry sleeping blanket and other trail items. A leather-covered tin canteen goes on the front. The rider's stirrups are covered leather and tapered for greater protection. They then buckle on leather leggings below the knees and put spurs on their home-made shoes. The quirt is tied to the ends of the reins; the rider swings it back and forth, slapping it on two pieces of leather that, once mounted, he drapes over his legs. These are triangular in shape and give further protection from anything that sticks -- which is just about everything that grows in this country.

41

So, with quirt raised high overhead, then brought down with a thud and a loud yell of "Burro!" we began to move out in a morning freshness of clouds that shadowed our movements across the top of the mesa. We would travel about a day and a half along the top of the mesas before starting down to the bottom of the canyons. We chose the longer route to connect up with the old Spanish trail over the mesa from San Inacio to the Mission San Bojas. This route was established by the Spaniards in the mid-1700's to connect and extend the chain of missions up the California coast. We came across Spanish crosses etched in stone to mark the highway which showed an incredible amount of use; the stones had been worn down four or five inches from the regular passage of unshod mules and burros over the centuries. Stone corrals, used for their overnight stops, still dotted the highway although it has not been in regular use since the time of the Spaniards, the natives having established new routes more to their present-day needs. No carts of any kind could have traveled the highway which at this point was just too primitive.

I kept getting an image in my head, as I gazed down this beautiful but rugged road, of over-sized Jesuits in Friar Tuck robes straddling under-sized burros and, with their little sticks, frantically tapping the animal's hindquarters to elicit greater enthusiasm for their journey down this Highway of God.

Heading for our point of descent to the canyons below and our final destination, our caravan passed through country guarded by thousands of giant saguaros, standing like a great army of soldiers brought to attention just for our passing. They were exceptionally fat and green, as all cactus are at this time of year after winter rains have helped brace them for summer's torturous sun and heat. Every color was richer as the shimmer of early morning dew made each bush and rock appear freshly painted as we rode by.

Two days later we arrived at the bottom of an incredibly beautiful canyon with tall palm trees and a clear, slowly moving stream that wound its way over millions of years of water-worn rock, creating its own abstract pattern. In some places the stream was only a foot wide, flowing into natural caches 20 to 30 feet wide. Clear water, breaking through its covering of lush green moss, was surrounded by time-polished white rock, with orange and blue dragonflies doing "touch and goes"

43

Changing Their Minds

along its surface. The ever-present background music of mourning doves echoed through the canyon walls. A brilliantly colored lizard scampered up a canyon crack for cover. A fly-catcher leaped for its dinner in the afternoon glow of the canyon floor. What a land of mystic enchantment!

Standing in the middle of all this kingdom of color and sound, we looked up and there was the largest cave painting in Baja. Over 75 yards long, more than 200 feet from the canyon floor. There we were, looking at a 900-year-old art show, spotlighted on the east wall by the late afternoon sunlight. Twelve-foot-high figures of human form, half black, half orange, with arms reaching toward the sky, and deer, turtles, bighorn sheep and whales -- all were defined with amazing clarity along the walls of the cave as we grazed from our canyon floor vantage point.

We climbed, with our camping gear, up to the cave to spend the night, just as those unknown artists had 900 years ago. We moved to the far end, away from the paintings, so there would be no possibility of our campfire contaminating them. Looking at photographs of the paintings, we had wondered why the figures were standing with upstretched arms, how the artists had gotten the idea for that pose. Now, in the glow of our first campfire, we could see our silhouettes on the opposite canyon wall. So we stood up on the ledge, with our campfire behind us, stretched our arms over our heads, and there were the figures on the opposite wall in the same 12-foot scale as the paintings. We felt this was possibly the inspiration for the pose the artists chose.

44

45

El Cacariso Cave And Juan
Flechas Cave, 1384

AUSTIN DEUEL

Many paintpots, actually depressions worn in the rock of the cave floor, are still stained with the colors used by the artists. They must also have used the palm trees from below to build scaffolding to stand on while painting. At 6'3", I couldn't begin to reach the maximum height of the paintings from where I stood on the cave floor.

The paintings here are attributed to a general Indian culture of that time, but there is no record of a particular tribe in the area, so they are said just to have been done by the cave painters of Baja. The Indians did not live here all year long, having been purely nomadic. They passed through these canyons in the fall on their way to winter hunting in the mountains, returning this way on their spring journey to cooler country and the summer fish spawning grounds on the Pacific Coast.

These cave paintings were painted on continually for six hundred years as the Indians passed through these canyons to and from their seasonal hunting grounds.

We gathered around the fire in comradely fashion, waiting for our fresh goat to finish cooking. A taste for goat meat definitely has to be acquired, but fortunately we had all done so over the years so we were looking forward to our evening meal. After dinner and a little conversation, weary from our day's ride, we lay back and admired the millions of stars sparkling diamond-bright against the black velvet sky until sleep came.

As dawn began to break on the high rim of the canyon, the frogs' nightly debate slowed to an occasional whispery croak and our feathered friends took over, welcoming the new day to this magical spot with their joyful chorus. The clean air, cooled by the night, moved gently over our sleeping bags. We stood up and stretched, then gathered small pieces of wood to start a fire for our coffee. As we waited for the water to boil, we were struck by the cleanness and freshness of the air, and by the light that sharpened the edges of every plant, every object around us. Soon the frenzied sounds accompanying the birth of this new day began to subside. Looking down to the canyon floor we could see deep, clear pools of water framed in white, water-worn rock and lined with palm trees. It was like being an eagle soaring in slow motion; it touched your soul.

After descending we planned to move along the canyon a

Loading El Diablo

50

51

short way to see another cave, much smaller but home to some outstanding figures not generally seen in this area. Flecha Cave, so named by Dr. Meighan, contained large figures with arrows stuck in some. These primitive St. Sebastian figures, painted red and black, suggested the Spanish name "flecha," or "arrow" cave. Among the figures were a large black deer, a red deer painted over a black bird, and numerous small figures. The cave is about 50 feet wide and 30 feet deep, quite small compared to the Gardner Cave a short distance away. We sat and enjoyed the cave's artwork and view for a while, resting from our arduous climb through thorny vegetation and steep, loose rock. But it had been a worthwhile struggle for these soul-searching moments.

Rested, we began our return to the base of Gardner Cave where we bathed and washed our clothes in the clear pools of water, then lay naked on the smooth, white rock to enjoy the magnificent sights and sounds. We savored it with mixed emotions, aware that in a few years it would all change -- the land, the people -- as the area became more accessible to the outside world. Walking around devoid of any clothing, I felt the rock under my bare feet and the air moving freely over my body, and it was as though a time machine had wafted me back nine hundred years. I felt both spiritually and physically in tune with the environment and culture of that long-ago time when these great murals were created.

Gardner Cave is the most densely painted place in this most painted section of the entire range where these giant, realistic artworks are found. Larger than the nearby Flecha Cave, it's nearly 500 feet long and 40 feet deep. One end of the cave has a very low ceiling covered with figures of deer, bighorn sheep, rabbits, birds and whales. There is considerable over-painting which, at quick glance, forms a very interesting fabric-like pattern in orange and black. The paintings are well protected from weather and in excellent condition. Grinding holes, lined up on the stone floor of the cave, are still stained by the pigments ground in them so many years ago. Staring at these holes, I felt as if the footsteps of the artist were left behind to provide company for the many works of art.

At afternoon's end, we fashioned a spout from a palm leaf and pressed it to the rock at a point where water was pouring from the canyon wall fresh and clear. Thus we filled our canteens for the night's needs, then started our steep trek to the

cave in the last light of this great day, to spend another night with good friends and the great spirits of this magical land.

Next morning we awoke to clouds and mist, but we thought it was just the morning coastal fog and drizzle normal for this time of year. As the morning progressed, however, we began to realize that the mist was turning to rain. Then we noticed that Juan's face was etched with a concern we had never seen there before. It didn't take much thought on our part to comprehend our predicament should the rain continue growing heavier. Those rocks that looked so smooth and white, innocent as virgins, didn't just happen. This area had been a raging river countless times, and if the rain continued to increase we could be trapped for several days waiting for the seeming innocence to return.

We made a decision to go for it, knowing full well that with such a late start we were likely to be stuck on the trail with no shelter available that night. This was not the side of the canyon to be stuck on, separated from our main food supplies stored on the other side. We had intended to stay longer, but decided to get to a spot where we could move when we wanted to. An hour and a half later we were packed. The rain had slowed a little, but we were still worried and the mules were slipping badly as we started off. We were all quiet with concern as we started up the canyon wall after a time of maneuvering along the canyon floor watching the stream show a constant increase in its flow. We were glad to leave the danger behind, and felt we'd be all right as long as the trail didn't get any wetter. The rain was slowing now, and after a while the sun began moving in and out as the storm clouds broke. The day was going to be nice after all.

In the late afternoon -- actually, almost evening -- we approached San Gregorio, located in the isolated northeast corner of Sierra de la San Francisco. Having grown accustomed to riding through harsh, somberly hued land, we were startled to see bright green orchards appearing before us, along with small garden patches surrounded by hand-stacked rock walls and strung together by a series of small irrigation ditches. It was a vivid contrast to what we'd been seeing in a land seemingly unconquered by man. We passed through a grove of lime, lemon, orange and pomegranate trees, their shade protecting very healthy looking gardens of onions, garlic and other vegetables. But this "oasis" was not very lengthy, and soon we were once again on the rough canyon floor we had been traveling over most of the day.

As we came out of the orchards we noticed a flume stretched across the canyon, about ten feet above its floor. This was made of split palm trees to avoid damage from the minor storms that occur here from time to time, although it surely would not survive any major storm. This area is subject to what are called "chubasco" winds that can unroof a house, flatten crops and whip fruit trees bare, but seldom cause damage to ranches or the land. Animals can find shelter in caves or the lees of steep cliffs, and native plants and trees are so adapted that they can weather such storms without serious damage. "Chubasco" storms usually occur in the summer months.

But the "trombas," or cloudbursts, are another matter. Torrential rains fall on the nearly bare rock surfaces of the uplands, with little penetrating the surface. Great numbers of high mountain capillaries send the water cascading down the steep canyon walls in its destructive race for the sea. Water may run a hundred feet wide and twenty feet deep through the canyons, tearing trees up by their roots and loosening boulders the size of small houses, rolling them hundreds of feet to stop only when jammed together at turns in the arroyo or when the water subsides. Most ranches are built above the high-water level, and enough water is left in natural catchholes for people and their domestic animals to survive until they are able to repair their waterworks located in the bottom of these canyons.

A little farther along the canyon from the flume was the rancho of San Gregorio. We decided to camp by the flume,

58

Moving Out

59

Needed Encouragment

just out of sight of the rancho, thus satisfying our water needs for the next few days. In the morning we would go and pay our respects, then leave from the rancho for the caves we came to see in this area. We set up camp and had dinner, then sat around the fire, talking quietly, until it was very late. Suddenly we heard the distant thud of a brass bell which was obviously moving toward us as it became louder and was joined by the soft jingle of spurs. We strained our eyes in the extreme darkness for our first visual contact with the traveler. Soon the light of our campfire began to reflect off a string of fully loaded burros plugging their way along the rocky canyon floor which was treacherous enough in daylight, let alone on a moonless night. The rider soon appeared and stopped in full view by the light of the fire. You could see the fire reflected in his mule's eyes, making him look formidable to our upward glance. Juan and the rider conversed in Spanish for a while. There was a bundle of hay tied to the horn of his saddle that he had stopped to cut in the gardens below us, which accounted for the distance between him and his burros. The sound of bells was becoming very faint in the distance as the burros continued their journey up the canyon.

61

Dinner At Cueva Pintada

He made a handsome picture -- they are very good-looking men of dramatic mien. But he couldn't tarry and shortly there was the sound of unshod mule hooves in quick step echoing through the canyon, and the diminishing sound of the bells was lost in the song of the spurs jingling in their effort to catch up. The blackness slammed over them like a giant door, sending a shudder down my back as I realized I was witnessing the last act of an honorable era in man's history, one of his ever-changing periods of life-style and culture that follow in the wake of the unending journey of time. I thought about this long into the night, and gave thanks that I'd been able to experience this before it disappeared altogether.

The next morning we went to the rancho to have coffee and exchange greetings. A charming place, very neat and clean, it was located up off the canyon floor to avoid high water during storms. We all sat on the patio of the main house, enjoying its cool relief from the harsh sun. The rancho showed considerable evidence of a woman's touch, with flowers everywhere planted in any available container. In view off one end of the patio was a water *olla* surrounded on all sides by red and yellow flowers, with a pair of mourning doves perched close by above, cooing in the bright morning light.

Centered against this background was an elderly woman whose whole life was written on a face full of character. Dressed in black, with her hands folded in her lap, she was obviously a widow and her silhouette expressed great resolution. Her world beyond this front porch was surrounded by high canyon walls that had held off the outside world for thousands of years. Yet this world in miniature contained a wealth of personal experiences as complete as though she had the entire globe at her disposal. Her whole life, longer than average for this area -- her loves, births, achievements, disappointments, happiness, sadness, deaths -- could be viewed from this very porch! It made a tremendous impression on me to realize that even though I had traveled vast distances and seen many things in my life, I would never witness as much drama as had been condensed in this tiny world within a world.

Rancho San Gregorio has a small herd of goats, just enough for their personal needs. Income is derived from tanned hides and finished leather products that they sell to the outside world or to the other ranchers who bring them hides in quan-

tity. Below the houses, near the floor of the canyon, are numerous hand-made vats that have a medieval look about them. These hold the tanning solution they make from a local tree. They start the tanning process by immersing eight or more hides in limewater, a saturated solution of quicklime, for 15 to 20 days. The vats used for this liming treatment are usually chiseled out of soft bedrock close to a natural water catchment or spring. They are very conspicuous because the tanner must work and agitate the hides during their two to three-week soak, and after years of use, lime builds up all around the vats, often staining an area of two or three hundred square feet as if it all had been whitewashed many times. The lime itself is prepared by burning limestone chipped from local deposits. It is placed in kilns fired by mesquite or other hard wood. Once fired, the dehydrated lime is reduced to a powder by grinding on a large *metate*, a stone mortar, using a heavy handstone, or *mano*. The same lime, called *cal*, is used to convert cornmeal to the masa from which corn tortillas are made. When liming is finished, the hides are scraped with the dull back side of a knife, the hair is removed from one side and all the saponified fat and membrane from the other. Then they are rinsed in clear water for four or five days to remove the lime and various soluble by-products of its action on the raw hide. The hides are then immersed in a solution of tanbark in the home-made vats at the rancho.

The tanner makes his vats, or *tinas*, from the wood of palo blanco branches two to three inches in diameter, in a manner that's traditional in the region. First he builds a square frame on legs -- a sort of table without a top -- four feet to a side. The legs and crosspieces are mortised together and lashed in place with rawhide thongs. Over this frame a large cowhide (or two hides stitched and caulked together) is loosely slung so it collapses inside the frame and forms a great pocket. The edges of the hide or hides are then stitched to the frame with more thongs. When the tina is filled with water the hide is stretched taut and bellies down nearly to the ground.

Tanning solution is made by filling the tina with fresh-hewn chips of palo blanco bark and letting them brew for a few days in the water. Just before using the solution, the chips are bailed out, leaving a rich red-brown liquid called *tinta*, or ink. Actually, the lime-treated rawhides are started in a partially

65

spent tanning solution. For the first week or two they are manipulated frequently, about every second or third day, in order to insure that the tanning ink reaches all surfaces and penetrates evenly. After two or three months the hides are removed from the tinta and hung wet over cords strung between trees or posts. The oil from sea turtles caught in the gulf is rubbed liberally on both sides of each hide as soon as the liquid has finished dripping. The oil-lathered hides are dried for four or five days, then returned to the vat which has been filled with fresh, full-strength tinta. After a month they are pulled out for the last time and rubbed all over with turtle oil, a paste made of animal brains, or a mixture of the two. When thoroughly dried, the tanned hides are ready to be cut and worked into valuable leather goods for trade or export.

The final agitation is done by the tanner. He turns and re-immerses the hides, then drains the liquid content of the tina and re-oils the hides. This last operation takes about two hours. He carries the finished hides up to a house where he has a worktable and tools. Here he will cut the hide into pieces appropriate for making saddles, *polainas* (the leather leggings worn by every Sierra man), belts, shoes and whatever other trappings are needed by ranch men and their beasts.

67

Tanning At San Gregorio

After Juan and Poncho had paid their respects and exchanged news of the area, we left to seek out the many paintings in this region. On foot, we started down the canyon until we came to one of the small arroya feeding the main canyon and turned up it. We quickly came upon paintings in small caves. These caves were full of many smaller works of art, in excellent condition and very precisely drawn. We spent the afternoon enjoying this collection, climbing in and out of the caves.

Sitting in one of the caves, out of the hot sun, we looked back down the sunlit arroya and admired the vegetation growing in great variety for such a small area -- all shapes, some leafy, some spiny, tall and skinny or short and fat, with colors as varied as the shapes. The canyon walls resounded with the song of birds -- the cooing of doves accented by the call of the gambel quail to its covey -- creating an illusion of gentleness and tranquility. But the rocks are hard-edged and sharp, the plants full of thorns and spines, the terrain a challenge to movement. Those who live here -- animal, plant or human -- are of hardy character.

Toward evening we started back to our camping spot. As we passed through the orchard we saw a man from the rancho directing the daily irrigation water that had collected in the sump from the night before. The spring that supplies the sump is located a few hundred yards up the canyon where it comes from a split in the volcanic rock and soon disappears into the porous canyon floor.

Loreto Arce, being a member of one of the families given the original land grant for this rancho, came here in 1928 with knowledge of the area he had gleaned as a young man hunting and herding goats in the region. He discovered the spring, found hundreds of years before by the Indians and the reason for their many paintings hereabouts. Selecting a spot in the water-carved canyon some 200 feet wide and a thousand feet long, Loreto, his wife and children laboriously created two to three acres of productive land where there once had been only palo blanco trees, rock and brush. Water had to be piped a half-mile to this level terrain, so he felled palms, split them in two and hollowed the halves for flumes. He built trestles to support these and keep them out of the reach of season flooding. The whole system is a duplication of the agricultural practices the missionaries brought to peninsular Cali-

fornia before 1700.

When Loreto had gotten the supply of water to his level area, he still lacked earth for cultivation. To supply this he brought in mules and burros, equipping them with *alforjas*, which are open, rawhide pack boxes. He and his relatives scoured the slopes and washes to find every small deposit of soil, or even sand, which could be scooped out and put in the pack boxes. He also was confronted with the task of controlling the flash flooding that occurred from time to time, and of raising two to four hundred pound boulders from the deeper parts of the waterway to build a levee to protect the higher levels during future flooding. Gradually his two or three acres were cleared of their larger stones and surrounded with rock walls five feet high and four feet wide. He then brought his hard-won soil by burro back in leather hampers and created shallow but usable planting areas within the walls. Thus Loreto created one of the elaborate *huertas*, or orchard gardens, which may be found scattered throughout the peninsular mountains today.

We settled into another night of discussions around the campfire, exchanging opinions about our findings and experiences on this trip. It was to be our last night in these magnificent canyons for another year.

Morning came easily, as sleeping quickly presented no difficulty for us in this country. We gathered wood for our morning fire as Juan and Poncho left to gather up the animals which, even though hobbled, had had a few days to wander in their quest for food, so would take time to round up. The sun was exposing itself over the canyon rim when we heard the soft sound of brass bells, first in the distance and then growing closer. Soon Juan and Poncho appeared, waving their arms and shouting verbal commands to persuade the animals toward us.

We packed up for the last time, mounted our faithful steeds and began our journey to the summit of this great canyon. In single file we passed through Rancho San Gregorio one last time, waving at the children and adults. The burros are always in front blazing the trail, with much verbal command coming from behind. Most of the time they seem to know which fork in the trail to take, and when they do choose wrong, Poncho spurs his mule forward to correct their decision. The trails in and out of these canyons are steep and

narrow, and lead across ledges with 900-foot drops straight down. Sometimes we had to dismount and cross on foot, leading the mules, and there were places where you could smell their hooves burning as the mules fought for traction as they maneuvered the trail's formidable obstacles.

This was all very nerve-wracking for me at first. I had never had much to do with mules until these trips, but I learned very quickly that they are amazing creatures, completely unruffled by mountainous terrain. They place one hoof on top of a boulder, then the next may go down between two boulders. A horse wouldn't last ten feet here. Even compared to others of their own breed, these mules are exceptional. For example, trips down the Grand Canyon are made by 17-hand-high mules with a weight limitation of 175 pounds. In the Baja mountains I ride a little 15-hand-high mule carrying 250 pounds over trails and ledges a sane human being would hesitate to walk over. A mule is a "one-time evolution," produced by breeding a female burro to a male horse. This pairing achieves the sure-footedness of the little burro and the larger size of the horse. Mules cannot reproduce themselves, but their value in this terrain is incalculable, and it's little wonder these mountain people consider mules to be their most prized possessions.

El Diablo

73

Heading For The Bottom

We continued our struggle for the top, resting every two hours or so, and we gave the animals one midway rest with loosened loads and saddles. On the way up we passed the carcass of a goat that had been attacked by a mountain lion -- we must have scared him off before he could enjoy his meal. Along the trail are a series of gates -- actually just stacks of tree limbs -- to help control the passage of animals from the canyons to the mesas and vice versa. The lead burros just crash through them, knocking the debris off the trail, and the last rider through dismounts and restacks the limbs before riding on. Unusual way to open and shut gates, but effective for this country.

We work the rest of the day at the task of reaching the summit before dark, finally arriving at last light. It was a marvelous experience, looking back down at the scene of our achievement, then out over the Pacific Ocean at a glorious sunset. But as we enjoyed the last light on the mountaintops above us and the last sounds of a closing day, we remounted, as we had more riding to attend to and man and beast were tired and slow-moving. We rode in darkness now, with no moon to light our path, leaving all footing and direction to the animals' strong homing instincts.

As we approached the village of San Francisco, I began thinking to myself that this was what it must have been like coming home a hundred years ago, completely tired and in complete darkness. Our first hint of habitation was the smell of woodsmoke, heavy in the air. Then we passed some goats and then the dogs, but not a light of any kind was visible. Our caravan was riding between hand-stacked rock walls with palm-thatched houses rising behind them. We stopped in front of one and dismounted, feeling for the ground in the darkness and hoping that whenever we made contact our legs would hold our weight. Clinging to the saddlehorn a moment for added support, I stood up and looked around me, seeing more clearly than you might think in such darkness. We unpacked by the light of the stars, placing the pack saddles and saddles in a line along the top of a rock wall. We used lead ropes to guide the animals to the corrals, the white mules as highly visible as a lighthouse on a dark coastline.

By this time lantern light was coming from the house and a dinner stove was started. It looked like a western painting done in moonlight by Frank Tenney Johnson -- only I was

living it.

In the morning we started preparing for our final departure from this land where time had stood still. Juan and Poncho were from different villages but, since Juan was the senior of the two, we gave him all the extra food and supplies and he and Poncho divided them up to their mutual satisfaction. They in turn would take the food to their respective villages for division among their own people.

We said our goodbyes to the villagers, then Juan and Poncho escorted us to the airstrip and our planes. We packed our camp gear and souvenirs into our 20th century flying machines, did our preflight inspection, said our last goodbyes and climbed into our aircraft. As we started the engines, their noise shattered the peace and quiet we had known for so many days. Amid billowing dust and flying rock, we revved the engines and headed for the end of the primitive runway. The tethered windsock hung limp from lack of breeze on this clear morning, perfect weather for our flight. We lifted off and flew low over the village, wiggling our wings in a final goodbye, then raced away to catch up with the world we'd left. Our faces were sunburned, our arms cut and scratched, and the cholla spines embedded in our legs would only come out long after our journey, reminding us of this land of ways that are old but honorable, and an art collection that Sotheby's can't sell and the richest art collector can't buy.

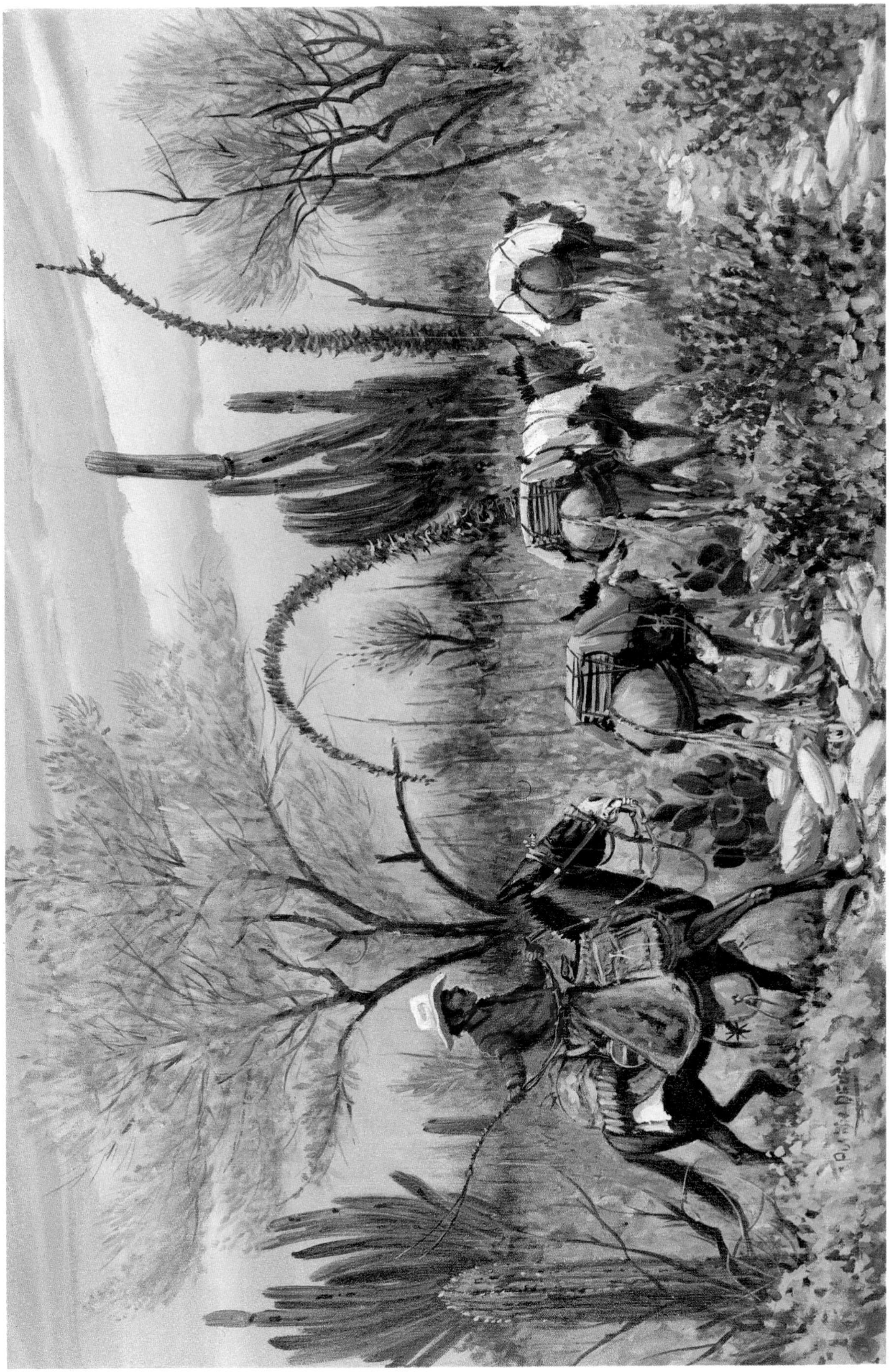

Boojum Tree Country

Fly Catcher

Gamble Quail

Morning Dove

Haffin Devel

80

BoJnm tree

Rostin devel

81

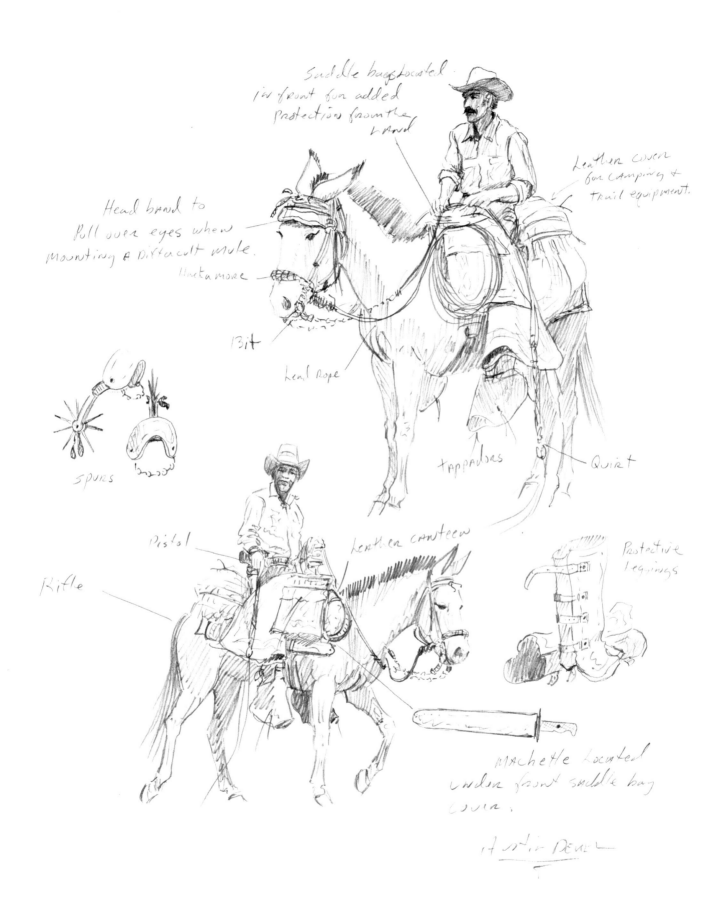

Saddle bags located
in front for added
protection from the
Land

Leather cover
for camping +
trail equipment.

Head band to
pull over eyes when
mounting a Difficult mule.

Hackamore

Bit

Lead Rope

Spurs

tappadars

Quirt

Pistol

Rifle

Leather canteen

Protective
leggings

Machette located
under front saddle bag
cover.

Austin Deuel

82

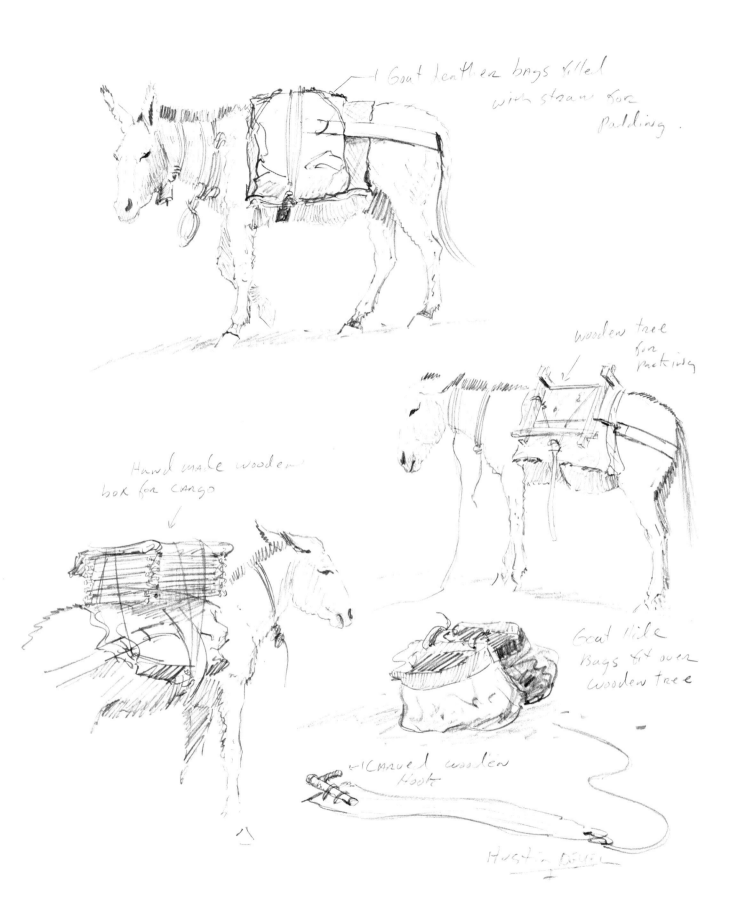

Goat leather bags filled with straw for Padding.

Wooden tree for packing

Hand made wooden box for cargo

Goat Hide Bags fit over wooden tree

Carved wooden hooks

83

PHOTOGRAPHS
OF THE
BAJA CALIFORNIA
EXPEDITION

85

BIOGRAPHY

Austin Deuel has won innumerable awards for watercolor, oil, and bronze sculpture in many major Southwestern art shows since 1966.

His work is in the permanent collection of museums from Canada to Washington, D.C. His work has also appeared on calendars, greeting cards and magazine covers for years.

While serving in the U.S.M.C., he served in Vietnam in 1967 as a combat artist. Some of these experiences have travelled with an art show in the past few years called "The Vietnam Experience" which has been well received in New York City and many other large cities in the United States. He was commissioned to do a heroic size bronze sculpture representing his experiences in Vietnam which is placed in the city of San Antonio as the Vietnam War Memorial.

CAÑON DE LOS ARTISTAS
EDITED AND DESIGNED BY GAIL CROSS
TYPESET IN SOUVENIR
PRINTED ON QUINTESSENCE DULL
BY
NORTHLAND PRESS
BOUND BY ROSWELL BOOKBINDING